Mary –
It was rad to read
with you at AWP16 !
So many well wishes for your
press .
        Friend + Far,
            AO

HOW LIKE FOREIGN OBJECTS

poems

Alexis Orgera

A Orgera

4/16

H_NGM_N BKS
www.h-ngm-nbks.com

FIRST H_NGM_N EDITION, APRIL 2011

ISBN 978-0-9832215-1-7

Cover photograph by Zsuzsanna Kilian
Book and cover design by Scott O'Connor

for Josh.

CONTENTS

Now do you see how in an instant the image
Falls from the edge of heaven to the edge of earth?

—Lucretius

HELLO, MY NAME IS SIGHING AURA

Goddamn, it's a blight outside
with the sun cajoling
the way it does when it's a fishmonger
or a cabinet breaker. Makes young girls
feel octagonal, the roar
of the city bus coughing out
dehydrated babies' breath. Ah, the man
with the F-O-O-D sign. He's a fucker.
If I ever go to hell I hope it's because
of my motherfucking mouth. And if hell
is a waterlogged shrew, perpetually
washing my tongue with Irish Spring,
then so be it. I like that first
taste of soap as much as the next
traveler. So clean, so blind
to the filthy state of the trash heap.
Sayonara, the driver said to me,
but I heard *Sighing Aura*,
and I thought,
what a nice way to put it.

STARGAZING

It's been said that dumb creatures
don't anticipate snow
or high winds off the coasts.
We claw and scratch
at the boat's horns—
we laugh in the mouth of the fire.
I went downtown yesterday
to buy my euphemisms, but
instead there were beasts, all manner of ugly words.
Beasts of the desert. Of towers.
Of fame. A movie star nibbled my earlobe
in the cauliflower aisle. Can you guess
how many years it took to grow
an appendage that tastes
like the nectar of movie stars?
My stomach's a race car
so I couldn't stay there long.
I am an ocean beast, if you need a label.
A rock dweller: green-lipped mussel
or a tidal snail. I like the sun.
I like the roar in my ears.

BEFORE THE FLOOD

The tub filled with pint-size titanics and bolshevik-
        red plastic jewelry
as I danced at the rumble of water, transported by rhymes:
        alexina, carina, birichina, bellina
wrapped in a towel of half-names which are the people
I almost became.

I'm left alone with a memory.

Whatever angel or snake whispered in my ear then
when I jumped from the tub and lopped off half my hair
        quick as a lost thought,
it closes its cellar door against the flood
where it hastens from whatever created it.

In my third year I was waterlogged,
ripe and half-bald, palming a ponytail-sized trophy
        in the other, more innocent hand.

ROAD TRIPPING

Trailblazing is a kind of murder, yet I'm trying to make you
into a proper place. We've crashed down
old state roads, self-satisfied wolves
who dig a trap from its moorings and laugh full of beef
at the unpacked dirt.

descending into into into...

The sky talks no sense but in terror,
in *anima mortal.* Dig a hole and you're there,
swallow a pill and you've found the mother lode, blow up
a tower—

I'm trying to make you into a proper plot of farmland
to grow my heart-sized radishes, my pole beans
and blooming lettuces so that I may camp under a sky
            that knows no boundaries
but atmosphere and classified documents.

I'll meet you for lunch there, call you my muse
sometimes, call you on the phone
which is a tin can and string
when the news is too much to believe.

I'll check the windows of your house, which is to say
the open air, for drafts or oncoming traffic.
I'll check your hair for beautiful noise
and pick the notes from the base of your scalp.

We're out in the open, specter.
We're like two field mice on a streetcar.

THE SOMNAMBULIST SISTER

When I was alone, you knew it.
Along the branches of this tree you saw me,
followed that weird timeline
against the violence
with a jalopy faith harbored
in your arms, your hands arranging
wide berths in the chaos. Your legs
kept you jogging on the vegetal rock
and brimstone air of a disenchanted skyline.
These were the songs
of our dog days, the ones we keep
turning back to like salt
nomads. We've walked that tensile rope
between reality and dream
with the sea legs of souls who were tricked
in childhood by old church hymns
and demi-truths dressed
as real porcelain dolls in a Lego field.
We're not the sleepers of the flesh.
Not the awakening of the spirit.
We count our sheep just like everyone
in the undercover pollution of night.
Let's have a reunion.
Meet me in the center
of our lives in that familiar, ghost-blistered dark.
Meet me with the legends we ate.
Bring the brick hallway separating
our bedrooms, the eternity it took to get
from one end to the other. Otherwise,
from what sulfur-fields will we ride out together
on the golden calves of our biblical past?

From what dancing frog-pulse
beneath oceans and craters will earth remember
our blueshift story—we the gliders,
the unbelievers, the archangels of unintentional glee?

HOW LIKE FOREIGN OBJECTS

Do I get to sit inside your mouth? she says.
And he thinks of her tongue as a waterbed
she's slip-sliding into him. She's an eel,
he thinks. A lovely electric blue
wriggling pinky. Maybe glow-in-the-dark
if he's lucky. Do I get to drink your spit? she says.
And he thinks of her swimming in a pool of vodka.
How drunk they'd make their somersaults.
How like foreign objects in their own skins.
Do I get to climb up your stalk? she says.
And first he thinks of Jack and his magic beans
and all the promises of the future,
but then he thinks of peeling bananas,
of greased poles, of the strongman competition
he will win when this is all over.
She needn't ask another question, ever.
But then she asks, Do I get to meet your mother?
Do I get to come home for dinner?
And what he sees is a flatbacked plank of oak
and three bowls of steamy chowder.
A coffin's worth of light in the crack
between her eyes. He sees how her questions
are really only the outlines of questions.
How gravity is what solders them glass
to glass to glass like the windows in church.

RAVEN COMES OUT OF RETIREMENT
FOR ONE NIGHT ONLY

A bellybutton swung from vines grown out of nothing—
discarded tools   a stone   a strap   a rod,
a trail of chipped bone bending into a place but not out—

has long since joined the myth-makers,
the flying tricksters   blues sung low cutting through us.

        If there ever was an eyeball here
I could still dig it out of night's thick clatter
clinging to the sides of ditches deeper than grown men.
I could still sculpt windowsill angels
from the red clay that only lives

in my head or in coquina shells spread
through flowerbeds   beneath roads that lead away.

But I can't. I haven't been back since I was a kid
to the burial grounds of the Waccamaw tribe,
there's nothing to shovel from their Place of Great
        Weeping except toenails and fingerbones and

the sneaking suspicion that somehow if I'd known
those great black birds
who could stand tall and walk like men,
        I'd have grown my beak wide as a flatbed
and sewn my wings broad, into the blackbacked sand.

THE REAL HISTORY OF THE WORLD, OR

Smack in the middle
of the situation we argued
for demographics. In a bar or the backseat
of a Honda or at a gravesite we spoke
gibberish or tongues or we didn't speak
at all, thinking loudly but opaquely
about the tired rooms we dwelt in.
Show us—we wanted to see candor-in-flesh—
where you stash all those megabytes
or phylacteries or tragic tabulations
of highway robberies, volcanoes
or knifewounds. We were talkers, alright.
Or intakers or sponges or curious
feral alleycats. We were early versions
of the videogames we'd become. No one
knows how to calculate the moment
when a person detaches from her body
to sing or dance or whatever
with Buddha or Mr. Rogers
or Duke Kahanamoku. Philosophy
is a seabird afflicted, like we are
in our dreams, with the ability to walk
on salt water which is buoyant—but still.
What everyone mistook for magic
all those years ago or alchemy
or sainthood or son-of-god
was a man on a surfboard. Even before
resin, before fiberglass, before slicking
through Pipeline's barrel, before waves
were ever named, before chasing the perfect ride
around this glassball oceanic playground,
there were slabs of koa-and-'ulu, wooden truths
on which to ride, so that being, say,

the savior of so many humans
or the owner of a dog
or a tower of strength
was simply a codeword for sliding
down the face of one extravagant yawn.

IMPERATIVE

So long as you don't miss the show—I don't care—
what I'm saying is, do whatever—

Pace the boardwalks filtering
bioluminescence through their slats

and the braided tide hitting a seawall,
smoldering in the deep cavern of a sailor's

chest where glowworms dawdle
and trade, where candles are wharves lit

with Chinese lanterns. Your forehead's
fireworks imprison you with supplemental

blackwash. It smells like varnish
all over the planet, and how the windows fog!

I know the noise of vehicles is deafening.
I know how much in the night sky.

Don't miss electron's fever radiating inward
like wake from a boat on the 4th of July

or the foliage of incandescence.
Don't miss a millisecond.

VIEW FROM THE THIRD FLOOR

> *Our mission wasn't to stop judgment day,*
> *it was to survive it.*
> —John Connor, *Terminator 3*

From my window in Boston I watch passersby
on Commonwealth gape at the hole outside
where a pear tree was. The way they lean
like skydivers into the December wind,
you'd think the end of days has dawned.
          All I want is for the world to end.

Like a prophecy we all remember:
And their eyes will run amok, one eye at this end of the world
peering into the ground, the other a floating tourist in the
Red Sea. So far away that an apocalypse here
means nothing there. I am dumb

from typing. This hole's impact alludes to hell
white noise   clear nail polish.
Truth is, only the starlings will find a way to freedom—
ice or fire, depending—

where they'll draw a NO VACANCY sign
in the clouds, leaving us heave-ho heave-ho
dredging the darkness below.

THE RED DRESS

My wedding day is a cliff
over a black, black sea.

Swirling sea.
Rocks-in-the-sky.

Men in Speedos jump from up here
into the water,

but the water
is so far away some men miss

and fall like discarded pants
to the volcanic rock

jutting in fists
out of the sea.

A body floats to the surface—
from up here in the empty

adobe church
I can see the surface

and I can see the body, jelly white
with black, black sores.

My dress is a red tablecloth.
The bridesmaids are strangers, small dark

women to whom I cannot speak.
I thank them

for joining my party,
and they nod and nod

and smile and all the while
those men are flying.

∞

You're never sure about the satin
pink camisole. Nor the party to which you'd
wear it. Nor the telepathy
of pets: knowing when you leave
the house they don't approve.
Nor possession by demons
even though it's all over
Discovery while you're getting ready—
the Texan priest in Mexico
calling out evil spirits from innocent
little muchachas, the occult investigator
in New England who finds herself battered
on the bedroom floor, possessed by a goat.
If a demon is anything at all,
it's a thing
that haunts the duodenum. Fear of talking
on the phone: demon. Desire
to drown in a clear pool: demon.
Love can be a demon, too. Look—
I won't always be here.
I won't want my boots muddied ad infinitum.
A woman sits in an office, equally
kelly green and bird's egg blue,
a triumphantly solved equation.
She wears the boots I was talking about.
If she were a speckled sparrow
I would talk about her in terms of bird fleas.
But no, she is the exoskeleton,
the experience outside, the opposite
of possession. A man tells her:
*It's your personal demons you need
to worry about, not those religious ones.*
By now, you're sure she is me,

and the office is my brain
telling me not to go to the party.
And the office is a voice speaking
inside me about all the things left
to do, the never-ending possibilities
of overcoming. And the office is the room
in which all of this fluctuates, peddles itself
into infinity. Like a symbol.
Like the thing itself, except not quite.

ON THE EXILE OF MY THROATS

Today we are sad—go figure—
like little enjambments we cry
for our lost intimacies. There's never
just one. They're fat rodents
skittering in the bamboo.
We are bullshark pissed at the losing,
we're creatures of mighty hallucinations,
of habit, of mostly latent risk.
I see my mate in the bed with me,
but in this nightmare of lost verity
he is a car length away.
His face morphs from full plate
to snake to so-small-it's-almost-gone.
What's the bitter pill I'm swallowing?
Little blue nervous-makers, tiny blenders
of burn. A reminder
that boiling isn't always the answer.
My mother taught me
to sauté when I was three. But then
I forgot and started boiling things
for their broths, and look what I got:
soggy, lecherous, makeshift eats.
A boiled onion is only a fraction.
A boiled grackle, a millimeter.
But that's so many years ago—
before words stuck
in my thirty throats weaving tender
tendrils from their vowels. Today
is another story altogether.
Today we are sad, me and my throats.
We wake up that way
after certain events we can't name.
I hear my throats cawing

through the window—I locked them out,
one thing leading to another
around midnight. They are meaner
than rooks, uglier than magpies.
My throats are a folktale
always throwing
their eyes into treetops
or spelling my thoughts inside out.

BEFORE TIME WAS A WAVE
IT WAS A CHILD

Their voices are seagulls. I am me but I'm a child–
I hear my parents call from across the department store,
all thirty years of me clinging to a clothes-rack, huddled
like a troglodyte to fit.

A weird displacement,

the kind you know will flee with the morning. I'm a speck,
too small yet to be real, too real to be theirs camped
in a battalion of flannels inside my own childhood
but sitting on a beach in Malibu here and now, split
down the middle. One half of a trochee
        like *human* or *crying* or *after.*

the sand, the waves.

My father calling, mother calling from far away as I hide
in Connecticut, December, a rack of coats in a crowded,
overheated store. They can't find me because I've grown
out of these clothes, growing tired of this game, of living

between these lines.

DON'T MAKE FRIENDS WITH HAPPENSTANCE

Happenstance has a way of shoving
that little square of paper
into your mouth, forcing a jig in the piazza
with fifteen palm trees swaying
to the gospel drone of your brain
while a mouthful of post-
teens strip and swell in the mud-
brick's night air. Happenstance steals
your verve, your verbal acuity
and fancies you a Cheshire shrine.
Happenstance takes a crayon
and draws your mother's birth canal
where you can't forget its tumbling
placenta on construction paper.
Little jay fallen from momma's nest.
There will always be
an eyeful of guilt—reading the wrong
novels while the posters on the wall
spill water from two dimensions.
Long after happenstance walks out,
closes the door, locks itself
away from the rest of adulthood,
there will be a flashy,
intense desire to meet God
in your armpit
one of those lonely nights
in college when just then, *just then*
you were the coolest kid
on the talking jungle gym.

SEE JUNE RUN

June is a better girl than July.
June has chipmunks
whereas July has black squirrels
in a graveyard. June has centrifugal force,
careening outward into the space
of all spaces, a room
full of delicate chaos. The briefest reprieve
from order, that June.
The smallest oxymoron.
July is a nutshell and cloying and wants
to stay close to home.
July is also a whirlpool.
But she doesn't know it.
July is dangerously close to spinning out
in a race from the center.
But she doesn't know it.
No one told her that physics doesn't
really exist, that force is just a name
we give to our own laziness,
that circles are just confused
straight lines. No one told July
about the blackness beating in her heart.
No one told July that her body
is not in a box, it is the box.
While June sits over the grave,
happy little campsite,
July suffocates on the particulates.

RECOGNITION STUMBLES INTO A BAR

so I say to Recognition: night is about the real stuff
of living!—This after an eclipse of dreaming
about many selves on a boat   all hymns
all guttural dresses   all weeping into the tin sea.
The myth of saltmaking unmasked—
which makes absolutely no sense to Recognition
in the condition Recognition is in

so I turn to Darkness who's groping the bar
for a match: there is no theory of the self!
Just another dead self on I-10 east of Baton Rouge.
You were with me, Darkness,
when I left my eyes on that highway—
and Darkness nods off into his amber pint

and I climb onto the bar—Can't you hear
the old tin sea? Listen!
Every object becomes a ghost! A kimono
floating through space, faces lasered
onto canvas on a far wall, a computer screen
at midnight, a child hiding
beneath a comforter, a painting staring
at its painter, books! a lamp! a record player!
a sea cucumber! this satellite, vegetable world!

DEAR PARTICLE THEORY

Dear eyes,
dear scrap of light shoved from a deep somehow
        bounding to its source.
Dear illuminated manuscript glow-in-the-dark
        under the pillow
                of intervening space.
Dear newspaper ads given way to grocery lists: dear yellow
        highlighter.
Dear Descartes (but only if light really is a rupture in
        the cosmic plenum),
dear comic of my life. Bang! Pop! Fizz! You're gone!
Dear Empedocles who swan dived into Etna like a
        soda bubble, whose campfire burned
                inside the human eye—maybe still does.
Dear seizure,
dear hallucination,
dear optics of India,
dear Hershey's wrapper glinting, lain fallow,
dear field and wheat and stone.
Dear sun emitting and absorbing light on the field
        and from the field.
Dear Newtonian corpuscle, the anticipation of dots.
Dear wave wave wave slip sliding from its momma.
Dear Einstein who sang: *Quanta, ride it home.*

Dear Lucretius, potion-drunk, straddling the interspace comet.
Dear big, big love.
Dear woman with night in your eye.
Dear pathos, and mirror praying that reflection bears
        a holy message.
Dear surviving everyday radiation.
Dear, oh dear, Moses parting legs like an infrared sea.

Dear bastard morning and whore Venus whose name in a far-
      flung language is *abhor dhei*, to very shine.
Dear How To Survive on the Surface of the Sun because,
      though you may get scorched,
                  you need the distraction.
Dear engine oil first gold as stellar piss and finally
      the fluorescent sludge
                  of a bazillion particles. Twinkling, twinkling.

POEM FOR THE TAKER

In conclusion, a man turned blue
right there in the backyard. He turned
blue and then the world did too.
So I'm giving up the ghosts
of blueness. We can't always spoon honey
into our eyes, parceling night into sweetmeats
whenever dead things rage at the door.
We can't always stick our fingers
in the cat's mouth. So I'm giving up
the ghosts. I'm giving up
the pine ghosts and the meditation ghosts,
the old pets who return and return
to their empty bowls, the dumb-limbed ones
playing at scaring a lonely girl.
I'm giving up the camera-
ghosts hiding behind my celluloid faces.
Giving up is hearing a voice you've always known
sing a song you've never heard.
If I wrote prayers on my tits
before I went to bed, it was because
I was sad for the singular
ghost some person always gives up:
Instead of thanks, she laughed in my face
and dared me to give her up.
My body moved in two retorts—
had I been an alembic
I might have found a way to distill the words
on my skin, but I am a giver of ghosts,
and these I bequeath to the taker of ghosts,
the master of spare parts
dividing his time between language
and dirt—long-toothed,
blue-devil, radiant native.

ILLUMINATRIX

A boy in Iowa suspects
three burning stars inhabit his chest
and gets lithium for his troubles.
The poet next door to him secretly
wishes the burn were his,
instead of a helium, bumbling heart.
A truck driver named Sally
up in Sacramento confides to a diner waitress
the sun's calling her future-name: *abuela, abuela*
from eighty miles off the coast
where a solar flare disturbs radio waves
all the way to Alaska,
and the aurora borealis takes the shape
of a firefly ten days running,
polar bears irradiated like orange lamps.

The Janus faces of incandescence scream:
Step Away From The Light.
To live life in a closet is to find peace
in stasis, like trans-filament meditation,
the incantation of a childhood rhyme
in a language I still don't quite get:
Nina o, nina o. Questo figlio a chi lo do?
—Who will we give you to?
If we give you to the laughing witch,
she will keep you for a week, fly you
on her broom, dropping stardust on the world.
If we give you to the black wolf, he will keep you
for a year in a cave, no fire, no sunrise.
And you will grow hard.
If we keep you for ourselves, we'll have you
forevermore under the blinding
light of the morning star.—

All this nasty effulgence reminds me
that across the States a father's light
dims, a mother's electricity sparks
and sputters like an angry vacuum cleaner.
Not news to anyone—
not to the rhythms of spectrums vying
for their fifteen minutes, petulant in rapid cycles,
not to the sky with its jewelry
caught up in our affairs,
not to the dancing picnics of flesh we call
like dogs into our lonely beds
to mask this infinite glare.

HURRICANE WARNING

Dear Alexis, we are calling to tell you the wind's
a wolf outside. There's a storm
out here, outside yourself. Outside of you
a template for accident, and inside too.
We're not lying. We don't believe
in luck. It's a myth that the right hand feeds the mouth
of the world. We believe in earth, as in silt,
water, as in salt bath, and unclaimed sins, which are daily
and inevitable. We believe in memory
only as a means to instigate disaster. For instance,
a man loses his memory and one day
out of the gaping remembers
that he's lost—what an apocalypse in his chest!
But Alexis, a spider crawled into your ear.
We saw it, and it laid its eggs in your ear.
This is not a legend. In the middle of the night
some day soon, you'll hear
the crunching sound of a dog pilfering
the potato chips inside your skull, and it'll louden
until you want to throw your head
beneath all eighteen wheels of a tractor-trailer.
Don't! The spider will crawl out now
when the rustling is at its worst.
Then you'll be free
of the cacophony everyone called
your imagination. Blake saw those angels
in the tree branch. Oh, he saw them alright,
and boy did he get a beating for letting on.
Alexis, don't let them beat you.
We called about the hurricane, but you may
predict that yourself, what with the oceans balmy,
jungles sucked bone dry and spewed out
again like lukewarm disciples. We called twice

and left messages. You didn't answer
or call back. Now we're worried
about your faithlessness in the face
of demolition. Alexis, what do you believe in
but sadness and circumference? How can you walk
in a hurricane and not get wet?

LIFE OF THE MIND

I've been a potato since the last time
it rained. In the dank I grow
pitiful and leathery, but I grow
nonetheless like a knot on a spine.
I can see a new heart sprouting
on my inner ear, beat
in the cupped chests
of quartz pebbles. Kerspark. Kerspark.
Something catches, a telegram
in the throat, a glowworm in dirt
and the night frogs find my heart-song,
learn to sing along, little
kaisers of the night, then coyotes
hear my song and holler—
And then the children out late marauding
hear my heart-song and they shriek
with mushroom delight, sucking
tiny fires into their lungs, blowing ash
from their own heart-studded eardrums.
But what's most strange in the dark,
in a dirt cell where the cold sits
on my eyes, is the sound of my own
heart beating from two loci,
like a drum circle it beats in my tuber head
then in my nightshade chest, echo
and echo and echo deprived of speech
but not of sound, a headlit train
in a tunnel under a river, muted
until it can't help but scream, screaming until
it screeches to a stop, forcing
the weight of thirst and hunger
into a pea-sized body
attached to the base of the brain.

My whole tumidity howls to its terminus
in the starless garbage pale.

IF ONLY TO WAKE WHEN NIGHT

Drive through the Mojave heading west
and you inherit the desert's hot breath
the parched sandpit of it—

When I was looking for relevance
I held hands with a world that needed me
badly as it needs fire trails

through lowland scrub,
root systems and laughter.

I was in a new kind of desert
where the Santa Anas lick down
your shoulders halfway through a latte,

but the Mojave's not duped
by orange blossoms, avocado trees,
clutches of Bermuda grass

when all irrigation gives rise
to twenty million fine, identical blades.

A city-desert is a nightmare world,
a Sahara sprawled in every direction
with stucco, brick, Spanish tile, sheet metal, glass,

teak and tile playhouses in the hills

where ficus and doum palms
        disguise the dunes,

where desert cars are hallucinations
across flats of broiled land

where women wear gauzy numbers to stress
their melon breasts and men hide
their bald heads in Dodgers caps.

When night breaks the sky is a starless
        fixed bluescreen
on the abandoned Dreamworks wagon,

but the city never sleeps,
instead it burns

with helicopter searchlight fingers
tattooing ten thousand lamps
of sand along my arms

only to wake when night's
a saguaro flower cloistered
in stout spines along the dry plains—

if the desert were a woman
she'd want to whistle a tune to herself
(you know what they say about a whistling woman)

lodged as she is in pancake rock layers,

      the millennial batter
of conch shells beaten

then cooked
      always wanting
always the mason of jettisoned architecture.

She would sing
through taproot fingers
      but the city wouldn't hear her.

SHIPWRECKED

Are you talking?
Because I can hear the breeze
clanking its purple ribcage
through a maze of coyotes.
Are the words calibrating
your lips into perfect hollows?
Typing is like talking.
Are you erecting ladders up, up, up
the building of your body?
Look outside.
The yard is emerald
but I don't know where I am
or to which coast I belong
when the race is done.
On my team there would be
t-shirts and bronzed ladybugs,
            water in perpetuity.
There would be a box
and far-flinging shadows
and two hundred tiny men
with their hearts ablaze.
That's where I belong.
On an island of organs.

THE PROBLEM WITH WARNINGS

Came home to three ships
who'd walked for days through fog
to warn me about the crow of distance,
but a recurring, deep black hole above my right eye
had already showed them enough–
so that when the ships saw me
they saw a Cyclops of the Angeles hills,
a woman in danger of being lit on fire
from the inside,
a diverticulate suicide.
They saw a woman covered in soot
and it frightened the wind from their sails.
For all the sailing they'd done
they had only seen dark harbingers of storm
in seabirds and black-
tipped makos, never a woman with a hole like an eye.
They didn't believe what they saw
so the ships conferred:
She is one black frog in an endless tree.
She is a vessel but not for sailing.
She has been sailed.

SLEEPING WITH THE DICTIONARY

I tell you what. It's never the definition
that makes its home in your underwear.

Nine times a man rides up to the house.
Nine times he's turned into a troll

for being obscure. Red handed he's defined.
Then again, this is the definition

of dissent. You have a hole to dig.
Your whole melts like the pencil sketch of a hole

over a candle's musketeer. Canopy:
Verb. To redeem the memory

of skin by knitting a forest's worth
of fingers around the heart.

Compilation: Noun. The place
where wrongs are filtered and shelved

like the idea of order on an island
you've seldom seen but floods with rum-

flavored lips and pelican-shredded T-shirts
in your dreams. Who said definitions don't matter?

Dictionary begs to differ. Duh.
He who never stays long on the same

word, amending his meaning
with every sweet-talking street vendor's

hand on his boxy ass. It'd be a shame
to find handfuls of old words

sewed into sweaty sheets. The alphabet
suddenly suddenly slow and slipping,

suddenly the outline of an angel sliding
its fingers onto my breast's modest definition.

THE TRUSTING, THE STUPID, THE DEAD

When I was a dreaming kid
I could close my eyes and trust
that outer space was a million incisors
chomping away at the void.
Even now, poking at my eyelids in the dark
I see computer-screen-blue and wonder,
Can anyone else see me glow?
When I was a stupid kid
Pepé le Pew nailed me to the floor
of a dumpster. Last night
was no different: a movie star shot rolled quarters
at a store clerk. My bank-robber
cousin vomited household appliances
all over her jail cell. Some days all you want
is to sleep and dream proper dreams
of going naked to school or flying
over mass-produced suburbs.
But mastering dreams is like raising the dead.
I won't lie. I'm laden
with birdcages holding babies with claws
and wings. Full of bayou graves.
When I close my eyes the chimera
wrangles for a place at the table. I'm stocked
to the gills with doppelgangers. In a world
dressed up in gradients of black and gray, I stumble
over toothy faces in the dark
like a gullible toddler, and what's worse is—
trusting and stupid and dead-sleep-walker
that I am—sometimes I recognize in them
the only radiant color left
in this whole goddamn universe.

CYTOKINESIS

All I can think is *where did she go?*
in the dark at 2 a.m., my heart racing
against its own Jungian synchronicity,
producing the memory
of fear, flashing a thousand pinhead
paparazzi cameras of the limbic system
when your plane's plummeting
at 40,000 feet or when your jacket
gets stuck in a ski lift mid-jump.
We don't forget those moments,
even in our sleep. What did I do
to produce in me this splitting—
self against self? *The son shall not bear*
the iniquity of the father, said Ezekiel.
But what about the daughter?
This is my father's fear
and his father's and all the fathers'
who ever stalked on two legs
across Europe for the mammoth.
We will not starve to death
nor will open oceans keep us
from sailing our outriggers to the land
that was birthed by the sun.
Take that, nighttime. I can see myself
on the opposite end of a room
which is now a panorama
of the room I'm actually in.
No light except what exudes
from both my bodies,
as if they are riddled with the light
of memory, the millions of tinny voices
that bind to receptors and scream,
Hey! Watch that cliff!

Hey! You're seeing a duplicate of yourself
in the dark! Scientists now imagine
that apophenia is the bridge between art
and insanity, whereas before it was just
the craziness of fitting squares
into circles and thinking all was patterned
in the world. I can see
myself, a paper doll
in a flimsy paper raincoat, the kind
with pinkynail tabs folded over
my shoulders and around my paperthin waist.
My other self, the one with me here,
in blue pajamas. Goethe saw his double
riding past on a horse
on the way to Drusenheim. The twin wore
an unfamiliar gray suit with gold trim.
When Goethe rode the route again later,
he looked down and realized the suit
he was wearing matched his doppelganger's
years before. Some of us can feel it happening—
a cleavage furrow forms
in the center of the cell and the cell divides,
and we watch ourselves running
away from ourselves in slow motion,
never gaining ground, convinced
we'll become the great philosophers of our age
if only we can make time move
backwards and reconvergence possible
in the schematics of the brain.

RULES OF GRAVITY

Darkness, like light, rises.
A lumberjack's axe.
Rises a scab,
a petrified ring of oak.
Rises in the heart of paleontology.
Rises in the barren water tank.
In the kettle.
On the fishing boat
from nets glinting
fins and marble eyes.
In the moan.
Rises from bed, whole.
Rises from the internal thermostat
of language. In quicksand,
rises up unafraid to feel,
to sound the conch
of serious discourse,
to pour water and believe in wine,
to find that gods
in the bodies of men are afterthoughts
of spontaneous praise.
That night ten years ago,
darkness was an awful tower.
It rose in you, old friend,
a nail to your wrist.
The two of us in my car,
darkness rose through bottlebrush
and Brazilian pepper
in the driveway
in droplets of blood.

Rose, an oubliette of mean fire,
through your body
then sank
a lodestone in me.

THE BLACK DRESS

It begins with a symphony growing
tendrils in the bathtub
or calls snails to dine in the cat's dish.

Every footstep gathers filth to share—

we discovered one night,
buckled into our corners,
that our house wanted a window's refraction

at just the right angles
        to start a flame,
to journey through fire and come out broken

but alive, so I hurried out in my famous black dress
to find wet logs for the fireplace,
and we became rodents in a smoking cage.

This was before you could ask a favor
of your house and watch it dance,
when some light was left to gambol through an Eden of dust.

ILLUMINATOR

1.

I found an illuminator of probability
who measures crescents

and symbols like equations in her calipers.
What's the likelihood of drowning, I asked her.

None, she said,
Your gills are the zenith of math.

A man with a fibrillating voice
sang into my left ear—

All around us, the ganglia of language
linked by synapse and spit.

We tongued each other's bodies:
two swells on a nerve fiber.

This was my dream of heaven.
A place undone by perfection.

But the world-game roiled below us.
Being a fan of the poetry

of the game, I cheered and wringed
my hands and, once, threw a glass of tea

at the screen. Night drew its shades
over the houses and still

I loved this game. The illuminator of arcs
answered via foghorn:

this is the closest you'll ever come—
don't let the light blind you.

2.

The illuminator of biblical
proportions shines her slim beam

on manuscripts and codices, papyrus
and goat-ball vellum, a letter written Christmas 1905—

annus mirabilis—in which Einstein himself
admits to no one that his dog howled

every last word he ever wrote: the dog
a reincarnated Empedocles

filling the water bowl with luminous parables:
As when someone planning a journey through

the wintry night prepares a light...
so did she give birth to the round eye, primeval fire.

In a rhubarb of jealousy, Al maybe killed the dog
with a fork. Here lies the danger

of harboring illuminators
in your bathtub. They drown themselves

with sadness. Again and again
the illuminator of melancholy, in her way,

understands paralysis. She wears
the shawl of it when nobody else will.

3.

Illuminator sounds like terminator sounds
like failure. We are failing

us. I am failing us.
I am flailing, hitting foul balls

into the body of water. I'm very proud
to serve on the board. Directors of illumination—

I don't illuminate, but sit
on the board—cracked pine—and wait.

Illuminator of termination sits here.
Illuminator of failure, there. There.

I'm still waiting for one of them
to rain on my one-wooden-bat

baseball game. I was a dynamic player once.
I could hit, I could run. I got the attention

of infielders and pitchers. All the resources
life requires, I had them in my glove.

But illuminator sounds like instigator sounds like
purloined letter. I could steal bases, too.

4.

And then the illuminator
of interstitial travel repeated:

All three furies are here!—
they'd followed Aphrodite from the genitals

of Ouranos, from bloody sea foam
out into the light—

The gods don't scare the seed from any man
So that he'll waste his life with a sterile Venus—

Like three doors on a game show
or the three spirits of a godhead,

pinholes of sky are easier to penetrate
than a body: *the space between*

sandgrains is safest, she said, *keeping you*
at the apex of your trek.

5.

Lighting candles to the illuminator.
We lived there, in that.

Mother and daughter, the gulf
and the gulf between, and the bay's mother

and the river's mother. The bay
which is never the river, in them

the danger of flood. Between the lumber
and lived. Then we built

gilded rooms: bog-prone guppies
we were. Built our house on stilts

according to flood's illuminator.
The origin of flood chases after

floodlight: its mother river rushing
to the river is the river never fire.

6.

At the transfiguration of the man
they called son, illuminator

flashed dark into day, cleaning up
botched deals and neglected dinner plans.

Illuminator drew blood from a thousand skulls—
being too close to the light

of the sun, everyone assumed
a miracle had occurred.

7.

I am afraid, dear illuminator,
to tell you the truth. I am afraid of the saliva

dribbling down my neck
and onto my breasts. I am afraid

you will laugh at me and call me
your bitch. I am afraid for you

to see me cry when someone's
father dies, not even mine, or when

a girl returns home after flying away
for a long time. A Greek said it best,

The sun throws back its light
towards Olympus with a fearless face.

But I am so human, so full
of naked parts.

8.

Illuminator of vision kicks
her legs atop the bookshelf. She's a laughing

quintessence in a babydoll dress.
She likes to ruin whole nights, to jab

sticks and pins into her humans.
She is jealous of other girls:

a couple hundred years back, she whispered
hysteria into a doctor's ear, and the rest

was a snug equation: if Aphrodite
fashioned the human eye

then did she also light the fire inside it
which shone out to illuminate desire?

9.

The illuminator's back today, sky
pulling like glue

over her massive skull.
She's bigger

than a thousand pages, encompasses
a city block. But she's in my arms, too.

And my ears, and she loves
to tuck my feet into bed at night.

Illuminator is an avocado pit
in the throat. She lives

to spiderweb our vision.
Why complain? she whispers.

Little cheek-golem. She knows
everything I own was hers first.

10.

You have trouble leaking
from your pockets, he said.

We were in bed together,
illuminator and me.

This was after he'd licked
my face, I'd spat on him,

he'd smacked me hard.
Ah, this is when life

becomes poetic, I said,
drenched and smarting

to the bone.

11.

Dear illuminator, we're bubblewrapped.
So bundled are we that we've grown

oxygen-pockets on our spines.
We sit at our desks during writing time

but can only listen: imagine
a world full of listeners: *the eyes shun*

things that dazzle, they flee the light.
Our fingers become

vestigial beings, wanting
only to feel the sea-air, to dig

into a lover's hair, to demystify silence.
Illuminator, we feel enormously concealed.

12.

So many illuminators to keep safe!
They move in half-moons and spirals:

churlish selves, muggled selves, wasteful
leaky-faucet selves. *It's easy*, they say,

for the earth to be stripped of light
And then to be filled and wash away the shadows.

You live on this orb
and they plow you into the thing

that you are, mix you up in a paint can,
desert you, return and bassinet you, pancake you

to the dirt floor, garrote you
with razorwire, bundle and tomb you.

They are mighty critics, illuminators, deft
in the art of finding meaning

where none should exist. We are,
all of us, looking out from our self-made cell.

13.

Dear illuminator, we have forsaken you!
We went to that place

where all land is desert
and the sand a leopard and our eyes

disarmed, and we were so busy
battling years of build-up;

so busy icono-graphing you
that we forgot you.

How sweet you taste; the way
your eyelids flicker

when you've been staring too hard
and too long at the world's screen;

your expanse amassed on canvas
like an alphabet

of still-beating hearts. Your edible
heart. How alone

in a roomful of sentence! We forgot
how to work, how to count our menageries.

Those sweaty particulates, the great
glassed-in forests you captured.

We're saddled to the tarmac
praying the plane won't ignite:

we need you, seedpod. We need you
our giant, refracted self.

14.

I didn't grow up in a barn
with the glissandi of two-note ducks,

the tessellated fracas of animalia,
but I've built a beauty right here

at the starting gun, red marginalia
melting the way it does.

The illuminator of daily
mundane mysteries draws a crescent

moon on a dirty dish. He says
it's goodbye, but I don't believe him.

Our midnight brannigans give us away.
We don't belong here, stories tiered

as they are and no light to read by.
Fists, the moons we always wished on.

The illuminator buys sixteen white mice
from a strip mall pet shop

and dismisses me from my post.
These, he says, *are my true people.*

BACK TO THE DRAWING BOARD

I drew a solitary revolving door,
made it a mad motherfucker possessed
of the millennium,
alone in a sea—
        I have drawn this door knowing
how soon I'll slide
from the smooth eggshell canopy
of earth—
        This door is my salvation
peddling along to scoop me up
when every last chance screams
to keep the stones
of memory safe—
        I drew this door into past lives
flying away from the pea-sized yard
of childhood where I am three or seven
or ten years old—
             a nun for Halloween
dressed by a Baptist
to piss off the Catholics.

I drew the door into the future
when the flack proves too heavy
to drag around—
           the door will say
remember you're sewn
from good cloth—

If it were a solid door
it wouldn't be time,
wouldn't progress—
If it were a mirrored door
and in the mirror ten thousand
unlikely angels,
superimposed photographs—
It would fill
with knobby tree roots
landing in my mother's womb
in the middle of a storm—
It would be truth
spelled almost backwards
and thirsty as hell—
but look!
I'm a baby in glass bassinet.
I'm a heartbeat—
now I'm gone.

THE DROWNING

One afternoon, a strange voice came home
sopping wet and blue-lipped,

hugged the dog so hard
I couldn't pry them apart

and this is what the voice told me:
           your fingers are electric

when you drown,
your lungs explosions

of port-wine stain.
Don't go, don't go, don't go, it said.

The voice made sense for a long time.

Then it went hoarse
and I missed it while I teetered on the couch

hoping this voice had found some truth,
a thing to change me

back to human
from the mushroom I'd become.

When the voice creaked again

it was a buffed canary,

a body washed ashore
on a beach with no shoreline.

Look how familiar this place is, it said,
the whole world a recollected song.

SUMMER VACATION

And you feel uncertain, not only about yourself, but
about the objects set there between you and another mirror.
    —Umberto Eco

You are you
            and I am I,
a flexing flame skimmer,
sinkhole cavorter.

Patience and cholera, my dear,
platitudes and pampas brooms,

and what I said to fifty other children
that day on the bus:

When I was your age I beat
the Coleman stoves piled high
against cinderblock walls
and clacked Budweiser cans
with my springbok jaw.

The Queen Anne loveseat
works to kindling left here,
the macramé rug hangs
on a floss line with the bleached bones,
            Lavoisier's mirror chimes.
I am here.
            I am not.

Today's mirage is an eye that catches
barred windows, shutters plastered
with L.A. Times from before the earth
could read.
                    I wore leather elbow patches,
thought I was the succulent Gobi.
That summer, my boots were an Alcatraz
and tongues of sand forgot my skin.

MOLTEN

I dreamed last night your name was Glass.
Not as in: I saw your name in glass
or I saw your name, and it broke
into tiny scintillas of name. No, I dreamed
in the fat heal of night, your name.
And it was Glass.
The name I would call you
if we could touch together
our index fingers and say Hello
like two sorrowful aliens
in this pelagic fortress.
Hello, Glass, I'd say. But there would always,
always be the danger of breaking
even though you are made of tremendous
pink cells and of glacial ice.
Especially dangerous is the danger
if ice when wind blows through its tunnels.
Another danger is scar. Another, choking.
Once, I watched a woman's face turn blue.
She was the arctic water of my dreams.
We hardly knew each other, believe it or not.
Glass is fragile but also beautiful.
I don't want to know
that you could have been Plastic or Plexi.
I don't want to know
the variations on Glass—except as the window
through which I see dissonance
and fasting, distant fire.

PLUMBING

Nothing works, but what doesn't work
most is the word *flesh* as in flesh,
my confidant, my cormorant.
As in flesh, my hometown. Flesh, lithe
neck of beach. Flesh my mother.
Flesh my flesh. Horror-ribbons
hanging from me in a dream. Never
a bottom to this pool I've been diving
for twenty-nine years. Never stones
or volcanic rock. Just swimming all this time.
Folklore knows that if you're a rag doll—
everyone is at least once—dangling
by a thread above all the hugeness
and travesty of landscape,
and should the thread break, should it pop
like an eardrum because it is not
eternal, it was never eternal,
close your eyes and water you'll become.
Water you'll ever be. Blue, fresh, breathing
flesh. Should this happen, let the water be
two hands, let them cup your eyes.
Let it be the place where you were born,
the womb you move into
and out of. Jagged place of bridging
syllables across whole countries.
Smooth belly of sand.
Place of pine sap but also sycamore.
Of honeysuckle but eucalyptus.
And tar. And noon. And paying for it.

STATIC

I fell in love one stormy summer
with a girl whose name
I don't remember. We rode bikes
in zig-zags as she sang
        jeepers creepers where'd you get those weepers…
I thought I would die.

In a lightning storm copperheads bushel
under our porch. We listen
with the ears of deranged bats
              for the static before the crash.
We listen all the time
for invisibles, an owl swooping,
demons coiled in the bedsprings.
            Anything.

In a lightning storm we rode,
stopping only to listen
for the electric pulse
that made the wet tar kneel.

UNLIKE MANY LAND MAMMALS

Until one day you began dying,
you were the bug of my life. To continue
this metaphor would be profane,
but remember that *bug* sounds like *love*
beneath the din
of iTunes across a long, narrow space.
We lived in an extra-long shoe-
box. We lived in the delinquent shadow
of bamboo. We lived as rats
clipped their nails on our walkways,
as humans screamed and punctuated
our infrequent lovemaking.
I am thinking of you in the past tense
to prepare myself for another day.
Reverse of psychology. More
akin to delusion. More like imagination.
More like swimming in a pool
that's turned green after winter.
I don't want you gone, mind you.
Far from it, I want to swallow you
and keep you packed in my stomach,
my humming dragonfly.
My nacreous friend on a cloudy day
or my conscience when we're both
up to our faces in it.

THE BRASS MENAGERIE

A girl uses her fingernails to gouge her name
into the credenza
where she's polishing a brass menagerie—

    In one sentence a whole lifetime

and inside it twelve hundred places to hide,
half of them in the forbidden
meadow where a farmer polishes
his gun: shot at her once
when she stole snappers from his pond—

    Twelve hundred places and counting.

A sharp knife's all you need in this life
        for snakes and men and mice
that swarm the hulls of grounded boats,
for scaling flounder, their biting
fins and slit bellies full of fine glistening eggs—

    To be present in the moment

of body filleted from consciousness,
to be the equation two halves solve
together, a vine breaking mid-swing
from canopy. If you count the hiding places
in the human brain

you'll find millions more
like tiny creatures skittering away.

WE DIDN'T GO TO SCHOOL FOR THIS

We decided to go miniature
one day when there was nothing left to do.
From the breadbox to the futon
we shrunk everything
to the size of our shriveled toes.
The way we held
our needle-forks at the knee-sized table
would have made our mothers cry.
We couldn't eat
more than a few bites
before our stomachs rebelled
the infant rations. But we kept at it.
Starving for our lofty goals.
The cat and the dog, each the size
of a child's hand, came with us
to the coffee shop where everything remained
normal, latte-sized and warm,
and stirred our imaginations—
maybe next we'd go giant, we thought,
swelling our bodies
and our wistful little hearts
to the size of city blocks, to blanket
the nakedness of smallness
we'd created in our own, self-
inflicted absences of girth. Maybe we'd go
big like the head of a pin
to a wayward atom.
We didn't know what we were doing,
did we, changing everything
but never changing enough,
walking through the maze of junk

we'd plundered.
But never slogging in the muck.
See the blue diamonds
on the back of that orange table?
Tell me those are not a map
of the disasters we've tooled.

SAILOR ON THE COAST OF BOREDOM

So I threw open the blinds,
lived a little, flung my body
from the balcony of the building
into the tar-water, to speak water
in a wetland where three generations of fishers
have netted their smelly dinners
and gone home to bathe in the blue light
of a corpse in the corner. And all the voices—
I mean all—corpses in the corner
of every living room in America
must have risen together
because the drone was deafening
underwater. I dog-paddled in the gullies
of incoming tide, one striped mullet
in a generation of bored fish,
escaped from the banks of the carnival
of our abandoned cities
into the cod-mouth of the Atlantic where
voices pilled in the brackish
swells as I floated very much alive,
the stars twitching in my wake.

CELESTIAL NAVIGATION

I'm on the green team trying to catch two moons,
grim, ungraceful, gargantuan things.

Don't leave me behind.
I'm belly up in a field of lightning.

If there's role call I'm collapsible, running with the canine
I'm invincible, plowing through the watermelons

I can dance on tiptoe.
Please remind me what gymnasium I'm in.

Remember my trisected tectonic plates.
One bruised apple in the fruitbowl.

Orion's grazing in the closet and tomorrow wheezes
in a semicircle whose name I'd kill to learn.

PALM READING AT THE ROSE CAFÉ

You will get a parking ticket on a Wednesday—
there's an angel of forgetfulness

in every car reminding you and reminding you
then pursing her lips into tight shoelaces

last minute. Angel of forgetfulness,
send this woman into the next world with a mind

wiped clear of parking meters. See this line,
this one here? When you are 47, you will stand up

in a restaurant and announce to the other patrons
that you will never again eat spinach.

This is the work of the angel of good,
green earth. She wants the roughage

for her compost. Tired of sharing her life,
her bedroom, her vintage hats. A big acceptance

is coming your way. It will make you
nervous and sorrowful. The line ends

there, but know you will be accepted which is half
the argument. We all remember which angel

orchestrates regret. Finally, and this is the last
line on your hand, but perhaps the most

genuine: you will own a white cat
and love it until you both die together

in a bed of variable, but believable, antiquity.
Angels don't care about cats. Nothing at work here

but time. Angels are mild
and middling, and only create worry-

lines on our faces because we look less
perfect. Then again, we look more like rivers.

THE OTHER FISHER OF MEN

To the water it slips into a tongue-tied golden ratio
        or a bog of mudworms
        or a gnat on the neck of the wineglass
left half-empty for a week.

The *it* is inexplicable, but it always slips away.

You follow it sometimes between urchins and seagrass,
up the mountains of oyster and bone and rock, sand that
buckles and shifts with the tides.

Your toes are always cramped after the search.

        Swimming in sweat, tendriled on a picnic table,
        two preachers anoint you
        and pray. Nothing

will change, the migraine will haul itself up
from its drowning to find you again
handing the devil his due in a fist behind the right eye.

It attracted big fish, this pain.

SEARCHLIGHT IN THE CANYON

In a round orbit revolves round the earth an alien light.
—Empedocles

Too arbitrary in the hunt.
Too much enthusiasm—turning over

the lone lemon lying
in the grass. Feces-studded,

leaf-worn yellow grass where all this
and other things are happening. Next door

blues rumble, and beyond that a woman
throws up into Tupperware, convulsing

to the slow rhythm of the Mississippi
grumble, and all those dogs!

with generic names who will eat you
out of boredom or some other human

instinct we're not sure we can name.
Nickel-hard deposits form

in the macula behind the eye
after years of worry, fornicating

with vision so that everything
outside this tiny box of flesh is a blur—

the men in black jumpsuits, the helicopters—
though their lights are limpid and bright.

If we all closed our eyes at once
this neighborhood would go black.

SAMSON IN THE GARDENSHED

You were down to the stones again
weeding up another goodnight.
        I thought I heard you say
Sheer me, love like some Samson
in the gardenshed
of my ribcage.

I thought your ghost troweled
under my skin
to sleep and dream and wave its hands
at the cogent demons
        that make us feel
like the drowningest plants
in a burning city.

I thought your breath siddharthic—
after all, that's what people do,
they breathe.
        You were not an irrational
irascible bag of pancreas,
liver, jawbone, Achilles heal

but an unexcavated ruin,
the seedling I was always seeking.

If your face changed into a stranger's in the dark,
I wanted to see you that way.

DON'T BE AFRAID, YOU'RE ALREADY DEAD

Everybody's talking backwards
just like in real life, pouring gallons.

A painter and a bluesman looking
for anesthesia at the bottom of a bottle.

Piss-drunk dad calls up his ex
to negotiate child support.

I have a problem with my hair
in that it keeps growing.

Been dreaming about drowning dogs
and crashing blue whales.

If the plane starts again out of the ashes
it's only because we know it should.

There's a control tower, a flight path,
darkness and light always in concert.

Some flooding in the rust belt.
People sweating.

A child sings, and that's where hell resides.
You're grounded, but one time you flew.

FALLING

There was some wabi-sabi between them,
and like cherry blossoms they fell

into bed. *There's nothing in me that's light*, she said.
He buried his head between her legs

to make her sing. But there was no song
in her. She was thinking

about the impermanence of motion.
He was thinking about the inescapable

nothingness he felt on Sunday afternoons.
How life is a series of light bulbs nobody uses.

A series of odd delinquencies called weekends
in which the ancient wabi-sabi drools between them.

FOLLOWING AN ELECTRIC ARC
BETWEEN TWO LUMINOUS POINTS

Wow look at that—the winking
lights of the lowcountry
fireflies, a transliteration
of the echo-dominoes packed into my ears,
repeating and repeating
You are, you are, you are here.
Even when you're not.
Night's a spontaneous biological order,
a series of synchronized flashes
in the dark, men with cigars
according to the Maya. I caught ten
in a pickle jar. Look, I squished their abdomens
onto my cheeks and eyelids and lips
and fingernails and secretly
onto the half-moon bottoms of my breasts.
Look, I've mimicked the *kunkay*,
ancient spirit of the ethereal.
The first firefly, queen of the stars.
The luckiest bug I know.
It's terrible, just being. No bioluminescence
to guide us. All that energy,
efficient and cool, converted into light.

DANTE IN SOUTH FLORIDA

This heat would scramble
even a gator's vision
building cathedrals of boredom
in a series of infinite vacations
        to hell, still as a seawall.

A plague of humidity devours
coconut palms like human heads.

Blue herons drill the mud
for shade beneath
        the raging eyes
of old growth mangroves
recording heat in an ecology of roots—

Heat is cousin to wildfire
and brother to no one.

Half aphonic, half demonic
not even the vernacular makes sense here
where the only cure is stillness
        edging us closer to paradise
on rattan armchairs
where we dream of our own
private, air-conditioned Beatrice

waving her perfect hand

through the Seminole mud
of centuries, the bathwater Gulf
and deeper and deeper
into Florida's dark teeth

　　　　where we'd sell our souls
for one second's cool relief
in that final lake of ice.

RETROSPECTIVE

Finally our city recollected itself
into trash heaps of racket, reduced us

to our essentials: hair, sound, and bone.
We rode the cobalt buses
as our less-vital selves and sang

in autobahn grocery aisles and sipped
a daily dragon soup that belied our hunger

for language. But a mass exodus drew scars
on the necks of hills. The moon eyed us
as we debarked our city

like possessed dolls, exonerating ourselves
from the noise.

We wandered outlying regions
where the lines between metal and pine
gouged deep wounds in the sand.

The city had tolerated our navels
for too long while we chatted on the phone.

She spat us out finally for running tepid,
decided to take back her stolen merchandise
and re-kindle the coarse fires

of mute discourse. Or did we choose to leave?
Our mothers taught us to look ahead

loudly, to define our plots by their baritone.
Our fathers gave us arrowheads
and whooped like caught loons.

They'd armed us for rebellion
but when we walked away

followed by complete and undiluted
stillness, we didn't know whose choice it had been.

We simply knew that here
was a dream of silence.

So we lay down our words,
littered meaning from our pockets
and left with scratches and scars in our eardrums.

We became a terra cotta army
out on the horizon between two worlds

deciphering the last whispers of our city
as we portaged our reed baskets
across a leeway of air.

DELAY INCLUDED

Has the world fallen to the tides,
the muscly-something-in-the-brainpan-as-liquid-

pulses-through barometers of mud?
Nothing but the calm

belt of nothing chewing our oars.
We're salty sailors in the lumen of the gate—

anticipate time where water is involved
and sink. We're waiting

like stranded clams for a plane to take us,
gypsy sailors on Christmas Eve

trying to get the hell home, doing the dead-man's-float
on the airport's wave pattern tile,

learning the only language of rapture there is:
Give away a pillow and we'll give you our slumber.

Give away a coffee and we'll give you ten fingers.
We'll lay down our oceans if you carry our bags.

EVENSONG

In the uncut gray
of pulled blinds you've become
something else—

        the bedroom's dirty secret—
        in a darkness bath, you and *not* you.

The galvanized metal dissolver of faith,
a half-life of afghan and dust mote.

No one peels away the pain
of two sickles in one eye, one blind eye.

Liar of air, migraine. Fakir of sound.
Twelve clicks of the metronome and you're done,
gone, flicked like a moth from the light of the sun.

        No one here is having fun.

Not living but breathing
beneath garbled pantheons
of laundrydrying, grassgreening in the heat

that gives way to the dew
which gives way to the drink
that only the tiniest creature tongues.

Nowhere near finished, this blocked passage
of cerebellum. Thank you, no,
says the ache behind the rightest eye.

I, oh righteous eye. Riotous above the clouds.

Your doppelganger speaks only to lie:
I am not the woman who made you feel the pain of this.

Not I, said the pain. *Not I,* says your twin.

I am not she. Not she-goat. She storm. She brave
atop the waves of circumferential silence
that does not exist

except in the head of the thing alive in your head,
that rears its ugly head
from the Venetian blinds, the blinding day-

light just like every other day,
helicopters blazing the shoreline.
Just like every other day, punctuated by anvil.

You know that death doesn't taste
like tablespoons of raw salt nor sewer nor rat

bludgeoned in the ear in the back yard
of peopleliving. It undulates,
coagulated oil on hot stones.

You are the Queen of the fabulatory moan.

An empty set of sleeves, a coercer
of smallness, darkness, and of easychairs.

You are someone else, and she screams
out of you,

Give me space and breath!
Don't leave! Don't leave! Come back
to sour smelling sheets

　　　—as if they're not your sheets—

to counting viscous sheep—
　　　though you've been counting sheep all day—
to my hollow-bleating, massive pleading bed—

　　　Your bed. Your unmade bed—

Come back green or hoarse
*or clown—*your nonsense—*come back with your woolen,*
stolen frown. Come back! Tell me

I'm no good—
　　　But it's you she's talking to—
I'm faking! I'm faking! Tell me that—
　　　But you can't, you know she's not—

But don't leave, but do.
Leave me counting upside down.
Leave me a history of women burned.

Tell me then that I'm a fake.
Leave me to the moth's pale light—
　　　Go have your life. Go have your night—
You'll come back!—

　　　And you will—

THE BLUE DRESS

Woke up thinking *she's in her dotage.*
I'd been dreaming about the blue couch
but was the couch on its final legs sequestered to a
living-

room with the untuned piano?

A woman can only explain her longing
for a blue couch by a trip to a psychic:

You were a whore the psychic says over tea and Oreos
*In your last life you were a whore and a handsome john
saved you from a burning building—*

You were wearing a blue dress.

So a woman buys a blue couch one sunny Sunday.
Light angling through jack pines and down again
through vertical strips of blind

into my childhood living room dangling
strange couchlike shadows around my arms.
        The couch slogged
across the Atlantic on the heels of its dark claw-feet.

Maybe it was going home and taking me with it.
Was I in my dotage?

The couch stared down the eye of a hurricane.
The couch carried my goose egg across the wild.

ACKNOWLEDGEMENTS

"Hello, My Name is Sighing Aura," "Imperative," "Dear Particle Theory," "Illuminatrix," "Illuminator," "Searchlight in the Canyon," and "Falling" were previously published in the chapbook, *Illuminatrix* (Forklift Ink., 2009).

Thanks to the editors of *DIAGRAM*, *Eleven Eleven*, *Folio*, *Forklift, Ohio*, *Fou*, *Free Lunch*, *Green Mountains Review*, *H_NGM_N*, *The Journal*, *jubilat*, *No Tell Motel*, *Planologie Blog*, *The Rialto*, *Sixth Finch*, *So to Speak*, *SUB-LIT*, and *The Tusculum Review* for first publishing many of the poems here, sometimes in different forms.

"Falling" was reprinted in *PANK*.

Thanks to the Dorothy Sargent Rosenberg Memorial Fund.

Thanks for Every. Single. Thing.—poetical and otherwise— Josh Grigsby, Rick Bursky, Matt Hart, Eric Appleby, Tricia Suit, Russell Dillon, Sarah Maclay, Gail Mazur, Dan Tobin, the Orgera clan, Rachel Rosen, Adriel Harris, and Ben D'Aste Sims.

Deep thanks to Simone Muench and Dean Young.

Light years of thanks to Nate Pritts and the H_NGM_N BKS editorial board for choosing to publish this book, to Nate Pritts for his editorial finesse, and to Scott O'Connor for his lovely book design.

Alexis Orgera was born in Connecticut, raised on the South Carolina coast, and ping-ponged the last decade between Boston and Los Angeles. A graduate of Emerson College's MFA program in creative writing, she is the author of two chapbooks, *Illuminatrix* (Forklift Ink, 2009) and *Dear Friends, The Birds Were Wonderful!* (Blue Hour Press, 2009). She currently lives in Florida where she works at her alma mater, New College of Florida, and edits *New CollAge* magazine.

53650478R00073

Made in the USA
Charleston, SC
17 March 2016